FOUR SAINTS IN THREE ACTS

Gertrude Stein

FOUR SAINTS IN THREE ACTS

AN OPERA TO BE SUNG

INTRODUCTION BY CARL VAN VECHTEN

NEW YORK · RANDOM HOUSE

1934

First Printing, February, 1934

PRINTED IN THE UNITED STATES OF AMERICA BY
J. J. LITTLE AND IVES COMPANY, NEW YORK

DESIGNED BY ROBERT JOSEPHY

A FEW NOTES ABOUT FOUR SAINTS IN THREE ACTS

IN *that book which is generally referred to—and the reference is seldom queried—as* "the *autobiography,*" *Gertrude Stein has written: "Virgil Thomson had asked Gertrude Stein to write an opera for him. Among the saints there were two saints whom she had always liked better than any others, Saint Therese of Avila and Ignatius Loyola, and she said she would write him an opera about these two saints. She began this and worked very hard at it all that spring and finally finished* Four Saints *and gave it to Virgil Thomson to put to music. He did. And it is a completely interesting opera both as to words and music."*

If I am correct, this happened in 1927 and Virgil Thomson put the finishing touches on the piano score in 1928.[1] *At any rate, it was in December 1928 that he arrived in New York from Paris with the completed score and asked me what he should do with it. I suggested that he might give an audition of the opera at my apartment when I would invite a few people who might be interested in hearing it performed. This audition was arranged, and one evening a little later Virgil played the score, singing all the parts himself, from beginning to end before this small group. Among those who listened were the sisters of Miss Florine Stett-*

[1] The work was orchestrated by Virgil Thomson during the summer of 1933.

heimer, whose baroque costumes and decorations were to become such an important integral part of the work as staged, and Mabel Dodge Luhan who made a remark which has become celebrated. "This opera should do to the Metropolitan," she said at the conclusion of Virgil's performance, "what the painting of Picasso does to Kenyon Cox." Somewhat later in the night, when Virgil and I were traversing the distance between two Harlem parties in a Rolls-Royce temporarily shared with us by an obliging fellow we had never seen before, I ventured to repeat this mot. The owner of the car was appalled by the possible implications of this threat. "Whatever," he demanded anxiously, "will I do with my Thursday nights?"

In the months that followed I heard Virgil play and sing the opera, or parts of it, on many occasions. From the beginning it has always seemed to me to be an extremely agreeable lyric drama, as original in its conception as Pelléas et Mélisande. *It stands alone, in fact. There is nothing else in the least like it. The rolling grandeur of Miss Stein's periods —for her language even in its most accordion-like shapes* will *roll along grandly—the humorous, colloquial interruptions are peculiarly suited to a musical setting. The music, in fact, is simple and moving, frequently ecclesiastical in style, occasionally mocking in its modulational manner, a perfect complement to the finely singable text which it always enhances and never obscures. This music is as transparent to color as the finest old stained glass and has no muddy passages.*

Nevertheless, despite my interest in and enthusiasm for the work, it did not seem likely that an opera for which there was so little precedent would find an easy production. It is doubtless true, however, that any worthy work of art seldom languishes long unheard in this world of ours, and so it did not surprise me too much when Virgil confided to me during the winter of 1932-33 that A. Everett Austin, Junior, had determined to open the new Avery Memorial Theatre in Hartford with the first performance of Four Saints. There are many persons in whose statements one has no confidence whatever, but Virgil is not one of these, and I believed that this was an event one could look forward to. A few days later he told me something even stranger: that Florine Stettheimer, one of the most vital and original of living painters, had promised to design the scenery and costumes. As Miss Stettheimer's reserve in regard to her painting has seldom permitted her to release any of her work even for exhibition purposes, I began to see that Virgil's powers of persuasion might be reckoned with in several directions.

Another important detail concerning the production was decided in my presence. Virgil had accompanied me to a performance at the Lyric Theatre in New York of Run, Little Chillun, Hall Johnson's choral play enacted by Negroes. It was, I think, during the intermission that Virgil turned to me and said, "I am going to have Four Saints sung by Negroes. They alone possess the dignity and the poise, the lack of self-consciousness that proper interpretation of the opera demands. They have the rich, resonant voices essential to the singing of my music and the clear enunciation required to deliver Gertrude's text." "But," I countered, "the opera is not about Negroes." "It doesn't matter," he retorted. "Think how many opera stars have *blacked up to sing Amonasro and Aida. Why can't my colored singers white up for* Four Saints?" *I could see no opportunity for argument here. Why not, indeed? Fortunately, in rehearsal it was found to be injudicious to resort to this device. The Negroes in their own persons proved to be more Spanish, more like saints, more even like opera singers than any group of white persons could have been possibly.*

For the opera was produced as short a time ago as last night—I am writing this on February 8, 1934—and in a manner so respectful to the formal elliptical style of its text and the simplicity of its devoted music that there could be no manner of doubt of its power to please. A performance of Four Saints in Three Acts—*incidently there are fifteen saints, excluding those in the chorus, and the opera is in four acts and a prelude—is a good deal like a dream in which you lie back indolently and let things happen to you, and* through *you, pleasant things to see, pleasant things to hear, pleasant things to feel. Possessed by a dozen contradictory moods in as many moments, you fall a prey to conflicting emotions and are at the mercy of author and composer. Such a passage as that of the wedding-funeral scene in the third act, with its sonorous music, its rolling, repetitive text, and its fine pictorial values, like a vast, sweeping canvas by El Greco, evokes compassion and pity. Such an episode as that in which the Commère and the Compère argue about whether they are going to witness the fifth or the sixth scene, or that other one before the curtain in which these two question each other—How many acts are there in it? How many saints in all?—are richly humorous. Then there are those unforgettable visions of the intricately strange prancing of the saints with torches in the second act or the ballet of the sailors and the Spanish señoritas in the third act, but to savor these one is required to attend an actual performance, as they form a part of the creative staging of the piece by Frederick Ashton.*

There are those, of course, who seek a key to some more perfect understanding of Miss Stein's text, just as there are those who wish to find representation in an abstract Picasso painting.[1] *It is unfortunate, perhaps, that I can have very little to say to these people. It becomes more and more evident to me that if appreciation of the text of Miss Stein is not instinctive with a person he never acquires it.*

A friend of mine who teaches school has told me that he had been asked by one of his pupils to write some sentiment in her autograph album. He chose to comply by inscribing his name under a familiar Steinian phrase: "Toasted Susie is my icecream!" During the recess hour he fancied the children were shouting louder than usual and he caught a more intense note of pleasure in their voices. Venturing into the courtyard he heard the cry taken up antiphonally: Toasted Susie is my icecream! Toasted Susie is my icecream!

In the case of Four Saints, *however, we are informed categorically by Miss Stein that she definitely set out to construct an opera libretto and in this connection I might inquire, dear reader, how many times you have heard Ponchielli's* La Gioconda, *how many words of the book your ear caught during any performance, how much Italian you*

[1] It was not accident surely that led the directors of the Wadsworth Atheneum, in which the Avery Memorial Theatre is situated, to give a Picasso show simultaneously with the production of the opera.

understand even when it isn't sung, and how much of the plot of this bloodthirsty fable you would be able to outline? If you are willing to face the facts, the chances are that you may discover that Four Saints *has the power to give you more pleasure—and a new kind of pleasure too—than that of any opera-book written in a foreign tongue.*

However, if you want Miss Stein's own description of her work, which may or may not help you to a further appreciation of it, here it is: "Gertrude Stein, in her work, has always been possessed by the intellectual passion for exactitude in the description of the inner and outer reality. She has reproduced a simplification by this concentration, and as a result the destruction of associational emotion in poetry and prose. She knows that beauty, music, decoration, the result of emotion should never be the cause, even events should never be the cause of emotion nor should they be the material of poetry or prose. Nor should emotion itself be the cause of poetry and prose. They should consist of an exact reproduction of either an outer or inner reality." [1]

If Virgil Thomson's music has perforce introduced an associational element into this prose, it has also "an inner and outer reality" of its own which stultifies this associational element and which perversely, but none the less with intention, has led to a rich and strange collaborative creation which very probably a future generation may be pleased to regard as a work of art.

CARL VAN VECHTEN

Hartford, Connecticut.
February 8, 1934.

[1] Page 259 of *The Autobiography of Alice B. Toklas.*

FOUR SAINTS IN THREE ACTS. *Words by Gertrude Stein, Music by Virgil Thomson, Scenario by Maurice Grosser. Performed at the Avery Memorial Theatre, Hartford, Connecticut, for the first time Wednesday evening, February 7, 1934.*

PRELUDE: A Narrative of Prepare for Saints.

ACT I: Avila: St. Therese half indoors and half out out of doors.

ACT II: Might it be mountains if it were not Barcelona.

ACT III: Barcelona: St. Ignatius and One of Two literally.

ACT IV: The Saints and Sisters reassembled and reenacting why they went away to stay.

CAST

— (all negroes) #

Compere — Abner Dorsey
Commere — Altonell Hines
St. Ignatius — Edward Matthews
St. Therese I — Beatrice Robinson Wayne
St. Therese II — Bruce Howard
St. Chavez — Embry Bonner

St. Settlement — Bertha Fitzhugh Baker
St. Ferdinand — Leonard Franklyn
St. Plan — George Timber
St. Stephen — David Bethé
St. Cecilia — Kitty Mason
St. Giuseppe — Thomas Anderson
St. Anselmo — Charles Spinnard
St. Sara — Marguerite Perry

2nd performance — Radio — May 25, 1947 —
All negro cast — mostly original #

Directed by Thomson —
in memory of G Stein.

St. Bernardine	Flossie Roberts
St. Absalon	Edward Batten
St. Answers	Forace Hester
St. Eustace	Randolph Robinson

MALE SAINTS

Harold Des Verney | Cecil Murray | Paul Smellie
William Holland | William O'Neill | Andrew Taylor

FEMALE SAINTS

Charlotte Alford | Lena Halsey | Olga Maillard
Dorothy Bronson | Sadie McGill | Cordelia Patterson
Josephine Gray | Assotta Marshall | Jessie Swan
Eva Vaughn | Alma Dickson

DANCERS

Carol Lynn Baker | Mable Hart | Maxwell Baird
Elizabeth Dickerson | Floyd Miller | Billie Smith

DIRECTION

Musical Direction	Alexander Smallens
Scenery and Costumes	Florine Stettheimer
Staging and Choreography	Frederick Ashton
Production	John Houseman
Technical Director	Kate Drain Lawson
Lighting	Feder
Chorus trained by	Eva Jessye

Mr. A. Everett Austin, Jr., President of the Friends and Enemies of Modern Music, has supervised for the society the arrangements for the production of *Four Saints in Three Acts.*

FOUR SAINTS IN THREE ACTS

Prologue - (Liturgical chants +

TO know to know to love her so.
Four saints prepare for saints.
It makes it well fish.
Four saints it makes it well fish.

Four saints prepare for saints it makes it well well fish it makes it well fish prepare for saints.

In narrative prepare for saints.

Prepare for saints.

Two saints.

Four saints.

Two saints prepare for saints it two saints prepare for saints in prepare for saints.

A narrative of prepare for saints in narrative prepare for saints.

Remain to narrate to prepare two saints for saints.

At least.

In finally.

Very well if not to have and miner.

A saint is one to be for two when three and you make five and two and cover.

A at most.

Saint saint a saint.

Forgotten saint.

What happened to-day, a narrative.

We had intended if it were a pleasant day to go to the country it was a very beautiful day and we carried out our intention. We went to places that we had been when we were equally pleased and we found very nearly what we could find and returning saw and heard that after all they were rewarded and likewise. This makes it necessary to go again.

He came and said he was hurrying hurrying and hurrying to remain he said he said finally to be and claim it he said he said feeling very nearly everything as it had been as if he could be precious be precious to like like it as it had been that if he was used it would always do it good and now this time that it was as if it had been just the same as longer when as before it made it be left to be sure and soft softly then can be changed to theirs and speck a speck of it makes blue be often sooner which is shared when theirs is in polite and reply that in their be the same with diminish always in respect to not at all and farther farther might be known as counted with it gain to be in retain which it is not to be because of most. This is how they do not like it.

Why while while in that way was it after this that to be seen made left it.

He could be hurt at that.

It is very easy to be land.

Imagine four benches separately.

One in the sun.

Two in the sun.

Three in the sun.

One not in the sun.

Not one not in the sun.

Not one.
Four benches used four benches used separately.
Four benches used separately.
That makes it be not be makes it not be at the time.
The time that it is as well as it could be leave it when when it was to be that it was to be when it was went away.
Four benches with leave it.
Might have as would be as would be as within within nearly as out. It is very close close and closed. Closed closed to let letting closed close close close chose in justice in join in joining. This is where to be at at water at snow snow show show one one sun and sun snow show and no water no water unless unless why unless. Why unless why unless they were loaning it here loaning intentionally. Believe two three. What could be sad beside beside very attentively intentionally and bright.
Begin suddenly not with sisters.
To mount it up.
Up hill.
Four saints are never three.
Three saints are never four.
Four saints are never left altogether.
Three saints are never idle.
Four saints are leave it to me.
Three saints when this you see.
Begin three saints.
Begin four saints.
Two and two saints.
One and three saints.
In place.

One should it.

Easily saints.

Very well saints.

Have saints.

Said saints.

As said saints.

And not annoy.

Anoint.

Choice.

Four saints two at a time have to have to have to have to.

Have to have have to have to.

Two saints four at a time a time.

Have to have to at a time.

Four saints have to have to have at a time.

The difference between saints forget-me-nots and mountains have to have to have to at a time.

It is very easy in winter to remember winter spring and summer it is very easy in winter to remember spring and winter and summer it is very easy in winter to remember summer spring and winter it is very easy in winter to remember spring and summer and winter.

Does it show as if it could be that very successful that very successful that he was very successful that he was with them with them with them as it was not better than at worst that he could follow him to be taking it away away that way a way a way to go.

Some say some say some say so.

Why should every one be at home why should every one be at home why should every one be at home.

Why should every one be at home.

In idle acts.

Why should everybody be at home.

In idle acts.

He made very much more than he did he did make very much of it he did not only add to his part of it but and with it he was at and in a plight.

There is no parti parti-color in a house there is no parti parti parti color in a house. Reflections by the time that they were given the package that had been sent. Very much what they could would do as a decision.

Supposing she said that he had chosen all the miseries that he had observed in fifty of his years what had that to do with hats. They had made hats for her. Not really.

As she was.

Imagine imagine it imagine it. When she returned there was considerable rain.

In some on some evening would it be asked was there anything especial.

By and by plain plainly in making acutely a corner not at right angle but in individual in individual is it.

A narrative who do who does.

A narrative to plan an opera.

Four saints in three acts.

A croquet scene and when they made their habits. Habits not hourly habits habits not hourly at the time that they made their habits not hourly they made their habits.

When they made their habits.

To know when they made their habits.

Large pigeons in small trees.

Large pigeons in small trees.

Come panic come.

Come close.

Acts three acts.

Come close to croquet.

Four saints.

Rejoice saints rejoin saints recommence some reinvite.

Four saints have been sometime in that way that way all hall.

Four saints were not born at one time although they knew each other. One of them had a birthday before the mother of the other one the father. Four saints later to be if to be if to be to be one to be. Might tingle.

Tangle wood tanglewood.

Four saints born in separate places.

Saint saint saint saint.

Four saints an opera in three acts.

My country 'tis of thee sweet land of liberty of thee I sing.

Saint Therese something like that.

Saint Therese something like that.

Saint Therese would and would and would.

Saint Therese something like that.

Saint Therese.

Saint Therese half in doors and half out out of doors.

Saint Therese not knowing of other saints.

Saint Therese used to go not to to tell them so but to around so that Saint Therese did find that that that and there. If any came.

This is to say that four saints may may never have seen the day, like. Any day like.

Saint Ignatius. Meant and met.

This is to say that four saints may never have. Any day like.

Gradually wait.

Any one can see that any saint to be.

Saint Therese	Saint Ignatius
Saint Matyr	Saint Paul
Saint Settlement	Saint William
Saint Thomasine	Saint Gilbert
Saint Electra	Saint Settle
Saint Wilhelmina	Saint Arthur
Saint Evelyn	Saint Selmer
Saint Pilar	Saint Paul Seize
Saint Hillaire	Saint Cardinal
Saint Bernadine	Saint Plan
	Saint Giuseppe

Any one to tease a saint seriously.

Act One

Saint Therese in a storm at Avila there can be rain and warm snow and warm that is the water is warm the river is not warm the sun is not warm and if to stay to cry. If to stay to if to stay if having to stay to if having to stay if to cry to stay if to cry stay to cry to stay.

Saint Therese half in and half out of doors.

Saint Ignatius not there. Saint Ignatius staying where. Never heard them speak speak of it.

Saint Ignatius silent motive not hidden.

Saint Therese silent. They were never beset.

Come one come one.

No saint to remember to remember. No saint to remember. Saint Therese knowing young and told.

If it were possible to kill five thousand chinamen by pressing a button would it be done.

Saint Therese not interested.

Repeat First Act

A pleasure April fool's day a pleasure.

Saint Therese seated.

Not April fool's day a pleasure.

Saint Therese seated.

Not April fool's day a pleasure.

Saint Therese seated.

April fool's day April fool's day as not as pleasure as April fool's day not a pleasure.

Saint Therese seated and not surrounded. There are a great many persons and places near together.

There are a great many persons and places near together.

Saint Therese not seated at once. There are a great many places and persons near together.

Saint Therese once seated. There are a great many places and persons near together. Saint Therese seated and not surrounded. There are a great many places and persons near together.

Saint Therese visited by very many as well as the others really visited before she was seated. There are a great many persons and places close together.

Saint Therese not young and younger but visited like the others by some, who are frequently going there.

Saint Therese very nearly half inside and half outside outside the house and not surrounded.

How do you do. Very well I thank you. And when do you go. I am staying on quite continuously. When is it planned. Not more than as often.

The garden inside and outside of the wall.

Saint Therese about to be.

The garden inside and outside outside and inside of the wall.

Nobody visits more than they do visits them.

Saint Therese. Nobody visits more than they do visits them Saint Therese.

As loud as that as allowed as that.

Saint Therese. Nobody visits more than they do visits them.

Who settles a private life.

Saint Therese. Who settles a private life.

Saint Therese.

Saint Therese. Who settles a private life.

Enact end of an act

Saint Therese seated and if he could be standing and standing and saying and saying left to be.

Introducing Saint Ignatius.

Left to be.

She can have no one no one can have any one any one can have not any one can have not any one can have can have to say so.

Saint Therese seated and not standing half and half of it

and not half and half of it seated and not standing surrounded and not seated and not seated and not standing and not surrounded not surrounded not not not seated not seated not seated not surrounded not seated and Saint Ignatius standing standing not seated Saint Therese not standing not standing and Saint Ignatius not standing standing surrounded as if in once yesterday. In place of situations.

Did she want him dead if now.

Saint Therese could be photographed having been dressed like a lady and then they taking out her head changed it to a nun and a nun a saint and a saint so. Saint Therese seated and not surrounded might be very well inclined to be settled.

Made to be coming to be here.

How many saints can sit around. A great many saints can sit around with one standing.

A saint is easily resisted. Saint Therese. Let it as land Saint Therese. As land beside a house. Saint Therese. As land beside a house and at one time Saint Therese. As land beside a house to be to this this which theirs beneath Saint Therese.

Saint Therese saints make sugar with a flavor. In different ways when it is practicable.

Saint Therese. Could she know that that he was not not to be to be very to be dead not dead.

Saint Therese must be must be chain left chain right chain chain is it. No one chain is it not chain is it, chained to not to life chained to not to snow chained to chained to go and and gone.

Saint Therese. Not this not in this not with this.

Saint Therese as a young girl being widowed.

Can she sing.

Saint Therese. Leave later gaily the troubadour plays his guitar.

Saint Therese might it be Martha.

Saint Louise and Saint Celestine and Saint Louis Paul and Saint Settlement Fernande and Ignatius.

Saint Therese. Can women have wishes.

Scene Two

Many saints seen and in between many saints seen.

Saint Therese and Saint Therese and Saint Therese.

Seen as seen.

Many saints as seen.

She is to meet her.

Can two saints be one.

Very many go out as they they do.

And make him prominent.

Saint Therese. Could a negro be be with a beard to see and to be.

Saint Therese. Never have to have seen a negro there and with it so.

Saint Therese. To differ between go and so.

Saint Therese and three saints all one.

Who separated saints at one time.

Saint Therese. In follow and saints.

Saint Therese. To be somewhere with or without saints.

Saint Therese can never mention the others.

Saint Therese to them. Saints not found. All four saints not more than all four saints.

Saint Therese come again to be absent.

Scene III

Could all four saints not only be in brief.

Contumely.

Saint Therese advancing. Who can be shortly in their way.

Saint Therese having heard.

In this way as movement.

In having been in.

Does she want to be neglectful of hyacinths and find violets. Saint Therese can never change herbs for pansies and dry them.

They think there that it is their share.

And please.

Saint Therese makes as in this to be as stems.

And while.

Saint Therese settled and some come. Some come to be near not near her but the same.

Sound them with the thirds and that.

How many are there halving.

Scene III

Saint Therese having known that no snow in vain as snow is not vain. Saint Therese needed it as she was. Saint Therese made it be third. Snow third high third there third. Saint Therese in allowance.

How many saints can remember a house which was built before they can remember.

Ten saints can.

How many saints can be and land be and sand be and on a high plateau there is no sand there is snow and there is made to be so and very much can be what there is to see when there is a wind to have it dry and be what they can understand to undertake to let it be to send it well as much as none to be to be behind. None to be behind. Enclosure.

Saint Therese. None to be behind. Enclosure.

Saint Ignatius could be in porcelain actually.

Saint Ignatius could be in porcelain actually while he was young and standing.

Saint Therese could not be young and standing she could be sitting.

Saint Therese could be.

Saint Ignatius could be in porcelain actually in porcelain standing.

They might in at most not leave out an egg. An egg and add some. Some and sum. Add sum. Add some.

Let it in around.

With seas.

With knees.

With keys.

With pleases.

Go and know.

In clouded.

Included.

Saint Therese and attachment. With any one please.

No one to be behind and enclosure. Suddenly two see.

Two and ten.

Saint Two and Saint Ten.

Scene IV

Did wish did want did at most agree that it was not when they had met that they were separated longitudinally.

While it escapes it adds to it just as it did when it has and does with it in that to intend to intensity and sound. Is there a difference between a sound a hiss a kiss a as well.

Could they grow and tell it so if it was left to be to go to go to see to see to saw to saw to build to place to come to rest to hand to beam to couple to name to rectify to do.

Saint Ignatius Saint Settlement Saint Paul Seize Saint Anselmo made it be not only obligatory but very much as they did in little patches.

Saint Therese and Saint Therese and Saint Therese Seize and Saint Therese might be very much as she would if she very much as she would if she were to be wary.

They might be that much that far that with that widen never having seen and press, it was a land in one when altitude by this to which endowed.

Might it be in claim.

Saint Therese and conversation. In one.

Saint Therese in conversation. And one.

Saint Therese in and in and one and in and one.

Saint Therese left in complete.

Saint Therese and better bowed.

Saint Therese did she and leave bright.

Snow in snow sun in sun one in one out.

A scene and withers.

Scene three and scene two.

How can a sister see Saint Therese suitably.

Pear trees cherry blossoms pink blossoms and late apples and surrounded by Spain and lain.

Why when in lean fairly rejoin place dismiss calls.

Whether weather soil.

Saint Therese refuses to bestow.

Saint Therese with account. Saint Therese having felt it with it.

There can be no peace on earth with calm with calm. There can be no peace on earth with calm with calm. There can be no peace on earth with calm with calm and with whom whose with calm and with whom whose when they well they well they call it there made message especial and come.

This amounts to Saint Therese. Saint Therese has been and has been.

All Saints make Sunday Monday Sunday Monday Sunday Monday set.

One two three Saints.

Scene III

Saint Therese has been prepared for there being summer.
Saint Therese has been prepared for there being summer.

Scene IV

To prepare.

One a window.

Two a shutter.

Three a palace.

Four a widow.
Five an adopted son.
Six a parlor.
Seven a shawl.
Eight an arbor.
Nine a seat.
Ten a retirement.
Saint Therese has been with him.
Saint Therese has been with him they show they show that summer summer makes a child happening at all to throw a ball too often to please.
Those used to winter like winter and summer.
Those used to summer like winter and summer.
Those used to summer like winter and summer.
Those used to summer like winter and summer like winter and summer.
Those used to summer like winter and summer.
They make this an act One.

Act Two

All to you.

Scene One

Some and some.
This is a scene where this is seen. Saint Therese has been a queen not as you might say royalty not as you might say worn not as you might say.
Saint Therese preparing in as you might say.

Saint Therese. Preparing in as you might say.
Saint Therese was pleasing. In as you might say.
Saint There Act One.
Saint Therese has begun to be in act one.
Saint Therese and begun.
Saint Therese as sung.
Saint Therese act one.
Saint Therese and begun.
Saint Therese and sing and sung.
Saint Therese in an act one.
How many have been told twenty have been here as well.

Saint Therese can know the difference between singing and women. Saint Therese can know the difference between snow and thirds. Saint Therese can know the difference between when there is a day to-day to-day. To-day.

Saint Therese with the land and laid. Not observing.

Saint Therese coming to go.

Saint Therese coming and lots of which it is not as soon as if when it can left to change change theirs in glass and yellowish at most most of this can be when is it that it is very necessary not to plant it green. Planting it green means that it is protected from the wind and they never knew about it. They never knew about it green and they never knew about it she never knew about it they never knew about it they never knew about it she never knew about it. Planting it green means that it is necessary to protect it from the sun and from the wind and the sun and they never knew about it and she never knew about it and she never knew about it and they never knew about.

Scene once seen once seen once seen.

Scene VII

One two three four five six seven all good children go to heaven some are good and some are bad one two three four five six seven.

Saint Therese when she had been left to come was left to come was left to right was right to left and there. There and not there by left and right. Saint Therese once and once. No one surrounded trees as there were none.

This makes Saint Ignatius Act II.

Act II

Saint Ignatius was very well known.

Scene II

Would it do if there was a Scene II.

Scene III and IV

Saint Ignatius and more.

Saint Ignatius with as well.

Saint Ignatius needs not be feared.

Saint Ignatius might be very well adapted to plans and a distance.

Barcelona in the distance. Was Saint Ignatius able to tell the difference between palms and Eucalyptus trees.

Saint Ignatius finally.

Saint Ignatius well bound.

Saint Ignatius with it just.

Saint Ignatius might be read.

Saint Ignatius with it Tuesday.

Saint Therese has very well added it.

Scene IV

Usefully.

Scene IV

How many nails are there in it.

Hard shoe nails and silver nails and silver does not sound valuable.

To be interested in Saint Therese fortunately.

To be interested in Saint Therese fortunately.

Saint Ignatius to be interested fortunately.

Fortunately to be interested in Saint Therese.

To be interested fortunately in Saint Therese.

Interested fortunately in Saint Therese Saint Ignatius and Saints who have been changed from the evening to the morning.

In the morning to be changed from the morning to the morning in the morning. A scene of changing from the morning to the morning.

Scene V

There are many saints.

Scene V

They can be left to many saints.

Scene V

Many saints.

Scene V

Many many saints can be left to many many saints scene five left to many many saints.

Scene V

Scene five left to many saints.

Scene V

They are left to many saints and those saints these saints these saints. Saints four saints. They are left to many saints.

Scene V

Saint Therese does disgrace her by leaving it alone and shone.

Saint Ignatius might be five.

When three were together one woman sitting and seeing one man leading and choosing one young man saying and selling. This is just as if it was a tube.

Scene V

Scene VI

Away away away away a day it took three days and that day. Saint Therese was very well parted and apart apart from that. Harry marry saints in place saints and sainted distributed grace.

Saint Therese in place.

Saint Therese in place of Saint Therese in place.

Saint Therese. Can any one feel any one moving and in moving can any one feel any one and in moving.

Saint Therese. To be belied.

Saint Therese. Having happily married.

Saint Therese. Having happily beside.

Saint Therese. Having happily had with it a spoon.

Saint Therese. Having happily relied upon noon.

Saint Therese with Saint Therese.

Saint Therese. In place.

Saint Therese and Saint Therese Saint Therese to trace.

Saint Therese and place.

Saint Therese beside.

Saint Therese added ride.

Saint Therese with tied.

Saint Therese and might.

Saint Therese. Might with widow.
Saint Therese. Might.
Saint Therese very made her in.
Saint Therese Saint Therese.
Saint Therese in in in Lynn.

Scene VII

One two three four five six seven scene seven.
Saint Therese scene seven.
Saint Therese scene scene seven.
Saint Therese could never be mistaken.
Saint Therese could never be mistaken.
Saint Therese. How many saints are there in it.
Saint Therese. There are very many many saints in it.
Saint Therese. There are as many saints as there are in it.
Saint Therese. There are there are there are saints saints in it.
Saint Therese Saint Settlement Saint Ignatius Saint Lawrence Saint Pilar Saint Plan and Saint Cecilia.
Saint Cecilia. How many saints are there in it.
Saint Cecilia. There are as many saints as there are saints in it.
Saint Cecilia. How many saints are there in it.
Saint Lawrence Saint Celestine. There are saints in it Saint Celestine Saint Lawrence there are as many saints there are as many saints as there are as many saints as there are in it.
Saint Therese. Thank you very much.
Saint Therese. There are as many saints there are many saints in it.

A very long time but not while waiting.
Saint Ignatius. More needily of which more anon.
Saint Ignatius. Of more which more which more.
Saint Ignatius Loyola. A saint to be met by and by by and by continue reading reading read read readily.
Never to be lost again to-day.
To-day to stay.
Saint Ignatius Saint Ignatius Saint Ignatius temporarily.
Saint Jan. Who makes whose be his. I do.
Saint Therese scene scene seven one two three four five six seven.
Saint Therese. Let it have a place.
Saint Therese Saint Ignatius and Saint Genevieve and Saint Therese and Saint Chavez.
Saint Chavez can be with them then.
Saint Ignatius can be might it be with them and furl.
Saint Therese with them in with them alone.
Saint Plan. Can be seen to be any day any day from here to there.
Saint Settlement aroused by the recall of Amsterdam.
Saint Therese. Judging it as a place to be used negligently.
Saint Ignatius by the time that rain has come.
Saint Genevieve meant with it all.
Saint Plan. Might meant with it all.
Saint Paul. Might meant might with it all.
Saint Chavez. Select.

Saints. All Saints.

Scene Eight

All Saints. All Saints At All Saints.

All Saints. Any and all Saints. All Saints. All and all Saints. All Saints. All in all Saints. All Saints. All Saints. All Saints. Saints all in all Saints. All Saints. Settled in all Saints. All Saints. Settled all in all saints. Saints. Saints settled saints settled all in all saints. All saints. Saints in all saints. Saint Settlement. Saints all saints all saints. Saint Chavez. Saint Ignatius. Settled passing this in having given in which is not two days when everything being ready it is no doubt not at all the following morning that it is very much later very much earlier with then to find it acceptable as about about which which as a river river helping it to be in doubt. Who do who does and does it about about to be as a river and the order of their advance. It is to-morrow on arriving at a place to pass before the last.

Scene eight. To Wait.

Scene one. And begun.

Scene two. To and to.

Scene three. Happily be.

Scene Four. Attached or.

Scene Five. Sent to derive.

Scene Six. Let it mix.

Scene Seven. Attached eleven.

Scene Eight. To wait.

Saint Therese. Might be there.

Saint Therese. To be sure.

Saint Therese. With them and.

Saint Therese. And hand.

Saint Therese. And alight.

Saint Therese. With them then. Saint Therese Saint Therese. Nestle. Saint Therese. With them and a measure. It is easy to measure a settlement.

Scene IX

Saint Therese. To be asked how much of it is finished.

Saint Therese. To be asked Saint Therese Saint Therese to be asked how much of it is finished.

Saint Therese. Ask Saint Therese how much of it is finished.

Saint Therese. To be asked Saint Therese to be asked Saint Therese to be asked ask Saint Therese ask Saint Therese how much of it is finished.

Saint Plan. Ask Saint Therese how much of it is finished.

Saint Therese. Ask asking asking Saint Therese how much of it is finished.

Saint Settlement
Saint Chavez } How much of it is finished.
Saint Plan

Saint Therese. Ask how much of it is finished.

Saint Chavez. Ask how much of it is finished.

Saint Therese. Ask how much of it is finished.

Saint Therese
Saint Paul
Saint Plan
Saint Anne
Saint Cecile
Saint Plan.

Once in a while.
Saint Therese. Once in a while.
Saint Plan. Once in a while.
Saint Chavez. Once in a while.
Saint Settlement. Once in a while.
Saint Therese. Once in a while.
Saint Chavez. Once in a while.
Saint Cecile. Once in a while.
Saint Genevieve. Once in a while.
Saint Anne. Once in a while.
Saint Settlement. Once in a while.
Saint Therese. Once in a while.
Saint Therese. Once in a while.
Saint Ignatius. Once in a while.
Saint Ignatius. Once in a while.
Saint Ignatius. Once in a while.
Saint Settlement. Once in a while.
Saint Therese. Once in a while.
Saint Therese.
Saint Therese. Once in a while.
Saint Ignatius. Once in a while.
Saint Ignatius. Once in a while.
Saint Therese.
Saint Therese. Once in a while.
Saint Therese. Once in a while.
Saint Therese. Once in a while.
Saint Plan. Once in a while.
Saint Ignatius. Once in a while.
Saint Therese.

Scene X

Could Four Acts be Three.

Saint Therese. Could Four Acts be three.

Saint Therese Saint Therese Saint Therese Could Four Acts be three Saint Therese.

Scene X

When.

Saint Therese. Could Four Acts be when four acts could be ten Saint Therese. Saint Therese Saint Therese Four Acts could be four acts could be when when four acts could be ten.

Saint Therese. When.
Saint Settlement. Then.
Saint Genevieve. When.
Saint Cecile. Then.
Saint Ignatius. Then.
Saint Ignatius. Men.
Saint Ignatius. When.
Saint Ignatius. Ten.
Saint Ignatius. Then.
Saint Therese. When.
Saint Chavez. Ten.
Saint Plan. When then.
Saint Settlement. Then.
Saint Anne. Then.
Saint Genevieve. Ten.
Saint Cecile. Then.
Saint Answers. Ten.

Saint Cecile. When then.
Saint Answers. Saints when.
Saint Chavez. Saints when ten.
Saint Cecile. Ten.
Saint Answers. Ten.
Saint Chavez. Ten.
Saint Settlement. Ten.
Saint Plan. Ten.
Saint Anne. Ten.
Saint Plan. Ten.
Saint Plan. Ten.
Saint Plan. Ten.

Scene XI

Saint Therese. With William.
Saint Therese. With Plan.
Saint Therese. With William willing and with Plan willing and with Plan and with William willing and with William and with Plan.
Saint Therese. They might be staring.
Saint Therese. And with William.
Saint Therese. And with Plan.
Saint Therese. With William.
Saint Therese. And with. Plan.

Saint Therese
Saint Plan
Saint Placide
Saint Chavez
and
Saint Settlement. } How many windows are there in it.

Saint Therese. How many windows and doors and floors are there in it.

Saint Therese. How many doors how many floors and how many windows are there in it.

Saint Plan. How many windows are there in it how many doors are there in it.

Saint Chavez. How many doors are there in it how many floors are there in it how many doors are there in it how many windows are there in it how many floors are there in it how many windows are there in it how many doors are there in it.

Changing in between.

Saint Therese. In this and in this and in this and clarity.

Saint Therese. How many are there in this.

How many are there in this.

Saint Settlement. Singularly to be sure and with a Wednesday at noon.

Saint Chavez. In time and mine.

Saint Therese. Settlement and in in and in and all. All to come and go to stand up to kneel and to be around. Around and around and around and as round and as around and as around and as around.

One two three.

There is a distance in between.

There is a distance in between in between others others meet meet meet met wet yet. It is very tearful to be through. Through and through.

Saint Therese. Might be third.

Saint Therese. Might be heard.

Saint Therese. Might be invaded.

Saint Therese and three saints and there.
Commencing again yesterday.
Saint Therese. And principally, Saint Therese.

Scene X

Saint Ignatius. Withdrew with with withdrew.
Saint Ignatius. Occurred.
Saint Ignatius. Occurred withdrew.
Saint Ignatius. Withdrew occurred.
Saint Ignatius. Withdrew occurred.
Saint Ignatius occurred Saint Ignatius withdrew occurred withdrew.
Saint Sarah. Having heard that they had gone she said how many eggs are there in it.
Saint Absalom. Having heard that they are gone he said how many had said how many had been where they had never been with them or with it.
Saint Absalom. Might be anointed.
Saint Therese. With responsibility.
Saint Therese. And an allowance.
Saint Settlement. In might have a change from this.
Saint Chavez. A winning.
Saint Cecile. In plenty.
Saint Eustace. Might it be mountains if it were not Barcelona.
Saint Plan. With wisdom.
Saint Chavez. In a minute.
Saint Therese. And circumstances.
Saint Therese. And as much.

Saint Chavez. With them.

An interval.

Abundance.

An interval.

Saint Chavez. In consideration of everything and that it is done by them as it must be left to them with this as an arrangement. Night and day cannot be different.

Saint Therese. Completely forgetting.

Saint Therese. I will try.

Saint Therese. Theirs and by and by.

Saint Chavez. With noon.

Act III —

With withdrawn.

How do you do.

Very well I thank you.

This is how young men and matter. How many nails are there in it.

Who can try.

They can be a little left behind.

Not at all.

As if they liked it very well to live alone.

With withdrawn.

What can they mean by well very well.

Scene One

And seen one. Very likely.

Saint Therese. It is not what is apprehended what is

apprehended what is apprehended what is apprehended intended.

Scene One

Saint Chavez. At that time.

Saint Ignatius. And all. Then and not. Might it so. Do and doubling with it at once left and right.

Saint Chavez. Left left left right left with what is known.

Saint Chavez. In time.

Scene II

Saint Ignatius. Within it within it within it as a wedding for them in half of the time.

Saint Ignatius. Particularly.

Saint Ignatius. Call it a day.

Saint Ignatius. With a wide water with within with drawn.

Saint Ignatius. As if a fourth class.

Scene II

Pigeons on the grass alas.

Pigeons on the grass alas.

Short longer grass short longer longer shorter yellow grass Pigeons large pigeons on the shorter longer yellow grass alas pigeons on the grass.

If they were not pigeons what were they.

If they were not pigeons on the grass alas what were they. He had heard of a third and he asked about it it was a magpie in the sky. If a magpie in the sky on the sky can not cry if the pigeon on the grass alas can alas and to pass the pigeon on the grass alas and the magpie in the sky on the sky and to try and to try alas on the grass alas the pigeon on the grass the pigeon on the grass and alas. They might be very well very well very well they might be they might be very well they might be very well very well they might be.

Let Lucy Lily Lily Lucy Lucy let Lucy Lucy Lily Lily Lily Lily Lily let Lily Lucy Lucy let Lily. Let Lucy Lily.

Scene One

Saint Ignatius and please please please please.

Scene One

One and one.

Scene One

Might they be with they be with them might they be with them. Never to return to distinctions.

Might they be with them with they be with they be with them.

Saint Ignatius. In line and in in line please say it first in line.

Saint Ignatius and friends. When it is ordinarily thoughtful and making it be when they were wishing at one time insatiably and with renounced where where ware and wear wear with them with them and where where will it be as long as long as they might with it with it individually removing left to it when it very well way well and crossed crossed in articulately minding what you do.

He asked for a distant magpie as if they made a difference.

He asked for a distant magpie as if he asked for a distant magpie as if that made a difference.

He asked as if that made a difference.

He asked for a distant magpie.

As if that made a difference he asked for a distant magpie as if that made a difference. He asked as if that made a difference. A distant magpie. He asked for a distant magpie. He asked for a distant magpie.

Saint Ignatius. Might be admired for himself alone.

Saint Chavez. Saint Ignatius might be admired for himself alone and because of that it might be as much as any one could desire.

Saint Chavez. Because of that it might be as much as any one could desire.

Saint Chavez. Because of that because it might be as much as any one could desire it might be that it could be done as easily as because it might very much as if precisely why they were carried.

Saint Ignatius. Left when there was precious little to be asked by the ones who were overwhelmingly particular about what they were adding to themselves by means of their arrangements which might be why they went away and came again.

It is every once in a while very much what they pleased.

In a minute.

Saint Ignatius. In a minute by the time that it is graciously gratification and might it be with them to be with them to be with them to be to be windowed.

As seen as seen.

Saint Ignatius surrounded by them.

Saint Ignatius and one of two.

Saint Chavez might be with them at that time. All of them. Might be with them at that time.

All of them might be with them all of them at that time.

Might be with them at that time all of them might be with them at that time.

Scene II

It is very easy to love alone. Too much too much. There are very sweetly very sweetly Henry very sweetly Rene very sweetly many very sweetly. They are very sweetly many very sweetly Rene very sweetly there are many very sweetly.

There is a difference between Barcelona and Avila. What difference.

Scene

There is a difference between Barcelona and Avila.

There is a difference between Barcelona.

Scene IV

And no more.

Scene V

Saint Ignatius. Left to left left to left left to left. Left right left left right left left to left.

When they do change to.

Saint Vincent. Authority for it.

Saint Gallo. By this clock o'clock. By this clock, by this clock by this clock o'clock.

Saint Ignatius. Foundationally marvellously aboundingly illimitably with it as a circumstance. Fundamentally and saints fundamentally and saints and fundamentally and saints.

One Saint. Whose has whose has whose has ordered needing white and green as much as orange and with grey and how much and as much and as much and as a circumstance.

Saint Therese. Intending to be intending to intending to to to to. To do it for me.

Saint Ignatius. Two and two.

Scene V

Alive.

Scene VI

With Seven.

Scene VII

With eight.

Scene VIII

Ordinary pigeons and trees.

If a generation all the same between forty and fifty as as. As they were and met. Was it tenderness and seem. Might it be as well as mean with in.

Ordinary pigeons and trees. This is a setting which is as soon which is as soon which is as soon ordinary setting which is as soon which is as soon and noon.

Saint Therese. In face of in face of might make milk sung sung face to face face in face place in place in place of face to face. Milk sung.

Saint Ignatius. Once in a while and where and where around around is a sound and around is a sound and around is a sound and around. Around is a sound around is a sound around is a sound and around. Around differing from anointed now. Now differing from anointed now. Now differing differing. Now differing from anointed now. Now when there is left and with it integrally with it integrally withstood within without with out with drawn and in as much as if it could be withstanding what in might might be so.

Many might be comfortabler. This is very well known now. When this you see remember me. It was very well known to every one.

Might and right very well to do. It is all colored by a straw straw laden.

Very nearly with it with it soon soon as said.

Having asked additionally theirs instead.

Once in a minute.

In a minute.

One two three as are are and are are are to be are with them are with them are with them with are with are with with it.

Scene IX

Letting pin in letting let in let in in in in in let in let in wet in wed in dead in dead wed led in led wed dead in dead in led in wed in said in said led wed dead wed dead said led led said wed dead wed dead led in led in wed in wed in said in wed in led in said in dead in dead wed said led led said wed dead in. That makes they have might kind find fined when this arbitrarily makes it be what is it might they can it fairly well to be added to in this at the time that they can candied leaving as with with it by the left of it with with in in the funniest in union.

Across across across coupled across crept a cross crept crept crept crept across. They crept across.

If they are between thirty and thirty five and alive who made them see Saturday.

Between thirty-five and forty-five between forty five and three five as then when when they were forty-five and thirty five when then they were forty five and thirty five when they were then forty five and thirty five and thirty two and to achieve leave relieve and receive their astonishment. Were they to be left to do to do as well as they do mean I mean I mean.

Left to their in their to their to be their to be there all their to be there all their all their time to be there to be there all their to be all their time there.

With wed led said with led dead said with dead led said with said dead led wed said wed dead led dead led said wed.

With be there all their all their time there be there vine there be vine time there be there time there all their time there.

Let it be why if they were adding adding comes cunningly to be additionally cunningly in the sense of attracting attracting in the sense of adding adding in the sense of windowing and windowing and frames and pigeons and ordinary trees and while while away.

ACT III

Did he did we did we and did he did he did he did did he did did did he did did he did be categorically and did he did he did he did he did he did he in interruption interruption interruptedly leave letting let it be be all to me to me out and outer and this and this with in indeed deed and drawn and drawn work.

Saint Ferdinand singing soulfully.

Singing singing is singing is singing is singing is singing between between singing is singing is between singing is.

Theirs and sign. Singing theirs and singing mine.

With a stand and would it be the same as yet awhile and glance a glance of be very nearly left to be alone.

One at at time makes two at a time makes one at a time and be there where where there there where where there.

Saint Ignatius. Might be why they were after all after all who came. One hundred and fifty one and a half and a half and after and after and after and all. With it all.

Saint Chavez. A ball might be less than one.

All together one and one.

ACT IV

How many acts are there in it. Acts are there in it.

Supposing a wheel had been added to three wheels how many acts how many how many acts are there in it.

Any Saint at all.

How many acts are there in it.

How many saints in all.

How many acts are there in it.

Ring around a rosey.

How many acts are there in it.

Wedded and weeded.

Please be coming to see me.

When this you see you are all to me.

Me which is you you who are true true to be you.

How many how many saints are there in it.

One two three all out but me.

One two three four all out but four.

How many saints are there in it.

How many saints are there in it.

One two three four and there is no door. Or more. Or more. Or door. Or floor or door. One two three all out but me. How many saints are there in it.

Saints and see all out but me.

How many saints are there in it.

How many saints are there in it. One two three four all out but four one two three four four four or four or more.

More or four.

How many Acts are there in it.

Four Acts.

Act four.

Encouraged by this then when they might be by thirds words eglantine and by this to mean feeling it as most when they do too to be nearly lost to sight in time in time and mind mind it for them. Let us come to this brink.

The sisters and saints assembling and reenacting why they went away to stay.

One at a time regularly regularly by the time that they are in and and in one at at time regularly very fairly better than they came as they came there and where where will they be wishing to stay here here where they are they are here here where they are they are they are here.

Saint Chavez. The envelopes are on all the fruit of the fruit trees.

Scene II

Saint Chavez. Remembered as knew.

Saint Ignatius. Meant to send, and meant to send and meant meant to differ between send and went and end and mend and very nearly one to two.

Saint Cecile. With this and now.

Saint Plan. Made it with with in with withdrawn.

Scene III

Let all act as if they went away.

Scene IV

Saint Philip. With them and still.

Saint Cecile. They will they will.

Saint Therese. Begin to trace begin to race begin to place begin and in in that that is why this is what is left as may may follows June and June follows moon and moon follows soon and it is very nearly ended with bread.

Saint Chavez. Who can think that they can leave it here to me.

When this you see remember me.

They have to be.

They have to be.

They have to be to see.

To see to say.

Laterally they may.

Scene V

Who makes who makes it do.

Saint Therese and Saint Therese too.

Who does and who does care.

Saint Chavez to care.

Saint Chavez to care.

Who may be what is it when it is instead.

Saint Plan Saint Plan to may to say to say two may and inclined.

Who makes it be what they had as porcelain.

Saint Ignatius and left and right laterally be lined.

All Saints.

To Saints.
Four Saints.
And Saints.
Five Saints.
To Saints.
Last Act.
Which is a fact.